WHERE LOVE TAKES YOU

AIRSHIP 27 PRODUCTIONS

Where Love Takes You
© 2017 Ron Fortier

Published by Airship 27 Productions
www.airship27.com
www.airship27hangar.com

Editor: Ron Fortier
Associate Editor and designer: Rob Davis

Marketing and Promotions Manager: Michael Vance

ISBN-10: 1-946183-07-5
ISBN-13: 978-1-946183-07-1

Printed in the United States of America

10 9 8 7 6 5 4 3 2 1

Where Love Takes You

An Original Stage Play
by Ron Fortier

HOW DAD MET MOM

An Introduction

In my life, I've yet to meet a single person who wasn't curious about how his or her parents met. As we grow up and learn the mores of our society, it is only natural that we begin to wonder at the love story that resulted in our very existence. Whereas most people eventually ask those questions of their parents, writers have a persistent need to know not only the tale itself, but all its details no matter how insignificant.

Such was the case with yours truly growing up in the small southern New Hampshire town of Somersworth in the late 50s and early 60s. Having been born in 1946, it wasn't long before I learned all about World War II and the resulting baby boom of the mid 40s after all those soldiers and sailors came home. I was one of the Boomers and quite honestly I relished the way in which Mom and Dad, in their own ways, would tell me about their first encounter, their early dates and eventually how it took a world war to break them up and almost curtail their love story. Each remembered similar scenes but in slightly different ways and it was left to my writer's imagination to edit the various incongruities into a smooth, cohesive whole.

Now I say that in referring to the shaping of the story in my mind alone. Early on the idea of writing the story was the furthest thing from my mind. But by the time I'd reached my thirties, and lost Dad at the young age of 59, a nagging obsession began to take over my life. Somehow I was driven to put down on paper the events as best I recalled them from their vocal narratives. I tried writing a novel and within a few chapters gave up. As prose, it just didn't come together. So what was left? A short story or novella? Neither format would work any better than the novel. Thus for many years I was stymied. I had a story but just didn't know how to tell it.

Then one day, early in 2001, while out for a Sunday drive with my wife, Valerie, the various incidents Mom and Dad had told me suddenly popped into my head aligning themselves in a set pattern as scenes on a stage. Honestly, it's a miracle I didn't drive off the road and kill us both. Such "eureka" moments are truly rare and I all but shouted out the words,

"IT"S A PLAY!!" My poor, confused Val looked at me as if realizing I'd finally lost my mind. I began to explain how, out of the blue, the answer to the riddle of my parents' love story had come to me in that instance of inspiration. It actually was a play and as such could be made to work.

If I could write it. Up to that point I'd written lots of comic books and fantasy action novels. But a play? Now that was a totally different beast. But I was determined to give it a go and within days, recalling those plays I'd read and studied in high school, I began writing what was to become "Where Love Takes You." It took two months to write. Val was anxious to read it and a bit annoyed when, upon its completion, I made it clear there was no way she would see it until the day it was performed on stage. She had no idea I'd put us both in the darn thing as the narrators. I've always loved Thornton Wilder's "Our Town" and the use of a stage narrator appealed to me a great deal. Good or bad, I wanted this play to be audience friendly. A narrator helps bring them more intimately into the tale as it unfolds.

And speaking of keeping it hush-hush, the one person I kept totally in the dark, along with the rest of my family and friends, was Mom herself. If I could actually find a company to produce it, I wanted it to be a big surprise for her. As it turned it out, it was just that, but never in the way I'd anticipated. You see, when we finally told her about the play, she became completely opposed to the idea and more than a bit angry with me for putting "her" story out there for all the world to see. It took Val and me weeks to calm her down and eventually make her understand my intentions were good. My parents are atypical of what genuine, down to earth people were all about in the Great Depression and the subsequent World War. My hope was that in their experiences, others would see their own love stories and future generations be given a glimpses into a more innocent age.

Still, technology would become my saving grace as I set about the arduous task of finding someone to produce it. Common sense dictated that I'd be wasting my time trying to find a large theater company. Rather I set my sights on seeking out small community theater groups the likes of which exist by the thousands throughout the country. These are wonderful creative groups with a sincere passion for theater and live performing. Thus, via the computer, I began my search and was ultimately led to an outfit called the Sanford Stage Company. Note, Sanford, Maine, was Mom's hometown and I hoped that connection might have some added appeal to this particular company. I printed out the play and mailed them a copy with a cover letter explaining its origin.

Then I promptly forgot all about it.

This was early in the Spring of 2001. Later, Val and I went off to Florida for a week's vacation in early Summer. Upon returning home, I discovered I had an email awaiting me from the Sanford Stage Company. It was written by one Mary Stair, a member of the company's overseeing committee and one of their directors. She informed me she had read the play, liked it and wanted to meet with me concerning a possible production. I immediately called her and we set up a Sunday afternoon meeting. Joining us at her home was another member of the company, David Goodwin. Both were excited about my play and confessed that they had never produced an original play before. They were nervous that they might be taking on more than they could manage. In the end, we agreed that the two of them, Mary and Dave, would produce and direct "Where Love Takes You," provided I joined their team as a story consultant. Both felt if I were directly involved with the casting and production, I could better assist them in bringing to stage the story as I'd wanted it translated.

And so began the casting call, sending out notices to various theater companies and local schools within a hundred mile radius of Sanford. Within a week we had both seasoned professionals and high school students showing up for auditions. And yes, I was there every single step of the way, watching people do readings from scenes and conferring with Mary and Dave as to who better fit the roles of my parents, my grandparents and family relatives. After two weeks we had a cast and a date was set for the actual debut. The company would do three performances between Aug 10 and 12 of that year. A Friday night show, a Sat night show and a final Sunday afternoon matinee. Rehearsals went off like a trip down a bumpy road and during the process I gained a much greater appreciation of what theater is truly all about and the hard work that goes into bringing any production to life.

On opening night, we filled the hall with family. No lie. It was also the second time many of these people had come together. The first time had been at Mom and Dad's wedding...and so here they were; the Richers and the Fortiers once again joining forces to bring something truly memorable to life. Mom was given the seat of honor in the front row, flanked by my siblings and their respective spouses. When the curtain went up and the young lady playing my Valerie walked out onto the stage, I held my breath and said a whole lot of prayers.

Then for the next two hours there was much laughter..and a few tears. A miracle of sorts had happened right in front of us and it became a magical night I will never forget.

Three days later, it was over and done. All that remained were the memories of actors playing real people and the audience who knew and loved those characters so much.

It's been over a decade since that one production and the play has never been done again.

People ask me if I'll ever write another and my answer remains a solid no. I'll keep doing the comic books and fantasy novels. But I would like to see the play resurrected and done again. Which is the reason for this copy you now hold in your hands. I still think its message is still one people want to hear. That when all seems dark and lost, love will always win out in the end. Mom and Dad proved that and so did millions of others. We should celebrate their victories and follow their examples.

Thanks for picking this up.

Ron Fortier
12/28/2016
Fort Collins, Co

WHERE LOVE TAKES YOU

A three act play

by
Ron Fortier

CAST OF CHARACTERS

The Fortiers

Ron Fortier—Author and narrator.

Valerie Fortier—Ron's wife and co-narrator.

George Fortier—Young man from Somersworth, NH. Is 21 when the play opens.

Richard Fortier—George's younger brother. He is 20 yrs old.

Raymond Fortier—George's older brother. At 23, he is the groom in act one.

Winnifred Sharpe—Raymond's bride in act one.

John Baptiste Fortier—Head of the family. A big, tall man.

Alphonse (Rose) Fortier—John's wife and the boys' mother. A small and feisty woman.

The Richers

Gabrielle Richer (gay-bee)—Beautiful 17-year-old girl. A carefree spirit.

Cecile Richer—18 years old, serious, practical sister and best friend.

Gene Richer—Girls' younger brother, is 15 at play's start.

Dorilla Richer—Girls' mother. A big, warm hearted woman.

Donat (doe-nah) Richer—Big, rotund man. Old fashioned bluster.

SUPPORTING CHARACTERS

Dance/Sanford

Emcee—Dapper fellow giving prizes at dance contest.

Henry—Young man who accompanies Fortier boys to the dance.

Alice—One of Gaby's friends.

Moe Bouchard—Young man infatuated with Gaby Richer.

Joe the Mailman—Affable fellows knows everyone in Sanford.

Billy Maddix—One of Gaby's neighbors. Joins the army.

Dr. Arthur Thompson—Local, well loved doctor.

Mrs. Thompson—Doctor's wife.

Father Lenoix—Catholic priest who performs both weddings in play.

Army Days/Los Angeles - Guadalcanal

USO Receptionist—Girl at front desk.

Cpl Armand Vachon—Soldier joining George for dinner with movie star Bing Crosby.

Bing Crosby—Well known singer & Hollywood movie star.

Ron Crandall—George's best friend in Guadalcanal. Helps him write letters home to Gaby.

All extras can double as family clan at end of play.

ACT I

(Curtain opens to reveal an empty stage. It is dimly lit.
A woman walks out from stage left and greets the audience. She is Valerie Fortier.)

VALERIE-

Hello. I'm so glad you could come to our play. My name is Valerie Fortier and the play is called, WHERE LOVE TAKES YOU. It was written by my husband, Ron Fortier, and I am very proud of him. In fact, today is Ron's birthday, so before we get started with the actual play, I'd like you all to help me sing Happy Birthday when he comes out. Okay? Great. Get ready now. Here we go.

(Valerie turns to where she first entered and calls out.)

VALERIE—Ron! Are you ready, dear?

VOICE FROM BACKSTAGE—Coming, Sweetheart. Be right there.

(Man appears on stage. He is wearing a cardigan sweater and in the process of adjusting his tie at the collar. He is the narrator, Ron Fortier.)

RON—Sorry about that. I was having trouble getting this tie straight.

(As Ron walks to her, Valerie turns to the audience and raises an arm to lead them in song.)

VALERIE (SINGS)—Happy birthday to you, Happy

birthday to you. Happy birthday, dear Ron, happy birthday to you.

(Ron stops and looks at the audience and back to Valerie, very moved by the unexpected welcome.)

RON—Aw, ...you didn't have to do that. I don't know what to say.

(Valerie steps up and adjusts his tie in one simple motion, smiling.)

VALERIE—Thank you, dear, will do nicely.

RON—Thank you, dear. Really.

(Valerie gives him a short kiss.)

VALERIE—You're most welcome, sweetie.

RON—I like birthdays.

VALERIE—I know you do.

(Hand in hand, they walk to the stage right front.)

RON—Do you know that if it had not been for World War Two, I would be four years older today?

VALERIE—Really. World War Two, huh? How so?

Ron—Well, you see, my parents met just prior to the start of World War Two and before they could really get their romance going, the war broke out and separated them.

VALERIE—I bet that happened to a lot of people.

RON—Oh, sure. But in my case it was different.

VALERIE—How so?

RON—Dad was much older than Mom and if they had not separated when they did, it is very unlikely their love would have survived, much less grown.

(Valerie takes a step back and folds her hands over her chest.)

VALERIE -
Really? Just how much older was your father?

RON—Dad was eight years older than Mom. When they met, he was twenty-five and she was only...

VALERIE—Seventeen. I see what you mean. That is a big difference. Especially where romance is concerned. Seventeen is still practically a kid. So tell us, what were the circumstances of this first meeting?

RON—Oh, that wasn't their first meeting. Well, it was and then again it wasn't.

VALERIE—If you're trying to confuse me, dear, you're doing it extremely well. What was it? Did they or did not meet like you said?

RON—Yes, they did. But they actually set eyes on each other four years earlier in a rather unique way.

VALERIE—Now this is getting interesting. Explain, sweetie, and please, don't leave out any of the details. This sounds like too good a story.

RON—Oh, believe me, it is. Why else would I want to set it down like this?

(Ron takes Valerie by the arm and escorts her to the left corner of the stage.)

RON—First let's set the background so everyone will have a better idea of where we are in the story.

(The entire stage area is lit, front to back curtain.)

RON—The year was 1938. President Roosevelt's government-created job organizations were slowly pulling America out of the Great Depression. In Europe, *Time*'s Man of Year, Adolph Hitler was nibbling away at the world map. In New York, the newest comic book craze was a different kind of superman. This one wore a bright red cape and defended the poor and the helpless. He was the creation of two Columbus, Ohio teenagers, Jerry Seigel and Joe Shuster. Congress established the first hourly wage at twenty-five cents and Spencer Tracy won the Oscar for his work in CAPTAIN'S COURAGEOUS only to discover the engraver had stamped his name, Dick Tracy.

(From stage right, two young teen-age girls appear, walking hand in hand.)

And in the town of Sanford, Maine, Gabrielle Richer and her sister, Cecile, were strolling the sidewalk on a quiet Saturday morning. Gaby, as everyone called her, was thirteen years old. Cecile was fourteen. They were among the first of ten children, my grandparents would have. Five girls and five boys.

(Lights dim on front and back, with spot on the two

girls talking excitedly. They are standing still.)

CECILE—So how much money did Mrs. Routhier give you for baby-sitting last night?

GABY—A dollar.

CECILE—A dollar! Lucky you. How much did Mama let you keep?

GABY—Fifty cents.

CECILE—Gee, that's enough to go see a picture at the State Movie House and then get a soda afterwards.

GABY—Why should I share any of this with you? You didn't earn it. I did.

CECILE—Maybe, but who helped you clean up the bedroom and get the laundry done so that you could leave right after supper? Come on, Gaby. You know Mama keeps me home helping her all the time and I never get a chance to baby-sit like you.

GABY—Oh, all right. Come on, we'll walk uptown to see what's playing. But if its one of those silly cowboy movies, I'm not going.

(The girls start walking towards stage left.)

CECILE—I heard its some kind of love story with Clark Gable and Myrna Loy.

(At mid-stage Gaby stops them and points to her front.)

GARY—Look over there. Something is going on at St.

Ignatius's. Look at all the cars pulling into the parking lot.

CECILE—Oh, it's a wedding.

GABY—It is! Who's getting married? Is it anybody we know?

CECILE—Uh-huh. It's Winnie Sharpe. You know, the nice people who live down by the hospital.

GABY—I think so. Isn't she tall and skinny and works at the Five and Ten.

CECILE—That's her. She's really nice.

GABY—Who is she marrying?

CECILE—Some French boy from Somersworth named Fortier. I heard some girls talking about it at the Post Office the other day.

GABY—No fooling! Winnie Sharpe marrying a French boy. I'll bet her folks aren't too thrilled with that, them being Irish and all that.

CECILE—Want to go in and watch it? I mean, we've still a few hours before the first show at the State and I want to see all the pretty dresses and stuff.

GABY—Okay. But we have to sit way in the back out of sight.

CECILE—GOOD. LET'S GO.

(Cecile grabs Gaby's hand and they rush off stage left. The lights dim after them.)

RON—Let me clarify that last statement my mother made about the Irish. When the French Canadians came down to New England in the late twenties and thirties they formed very tight communities and basically kept to their own language and customs. Since most were Catholics, they also established their own churches separate from the already established English parishes. For some strange reason, they referred to all non-French people as Irish.

Most cities and towns of the period thus had two very different and distinct parishes living side by side with each other like friendly strangers.

(Lights go up over center stage to see a series of folding chairs going across the stage. To the right rear are a raised platform and a small altar where a priest is getting things ready for the wedding.)

(Gaby & Cecile come in at stage left. They genuflect; make the sign of the cross then take two seats in the last row.)

(From stage right the groom appears with his father. The groom is nervously tugging at his tie, while his father nods and waves to the priest.)

RON—(Indicating the two men at stage right.)

There's my uncle Ray and my grandfather, John Baptiste Fortier. God, I'd forgotten what a big man he was. He's about to give Uncle Ray his patented be-gentle sex speech.

RAY—Geez, Dad, why do we have to wear these damn monkey suits? This damn stupid tie is strangling me!

JOHN—Hush, up, Ray. This is a church. Watch your mouth.

RAY—Sure, Papa. I'm just nervous, is all. Geez, I wish this would get started and be over with.

JOHN—Don't rush things, boy. You've your whole life ahead of you. Which is a good time to bring up something you should keep in mind.

(John puts his arm around his son's shoulder and walks him away from the altar and the priest.)

RAY—What Papa?

JOHN—This thing between a man and a woman...

RAY—Huh? What?

JOHN—You know what I'm talking about. The thing... the love...you know, tonight...on your honeymoon.

RAY—OH! Right! That! What about it?

JOHN—Don't rush it, boy. You know. Don't scare her or anything. She's a good girl and ...well, you and she have your life ahead of you. You don't have to get everything the first night.

RAY—Huh?

JOHN—Do you understand me, Raymond? Take it easy on your bride. Be kind and gentle. A good wife is God's greatest blessing to a man. Don't forget that.

(From stage left comes a small, gray haired woman with two handsome young men escorting her. She is Mrs. John Fortier and the men are two of her other sons, George & Richard. They stop at mid-stage as she spots Ray and Mr. Fortier.)

RON—There's my grandmother, Rose, and dad and Uncle Richard. They were ushers at this wedding.

VALERIE—I never realized your grandmother was such a small woman.

RON—She looked even smaller along side my grandfather. Yet she had six strapping boys and always was the real head of the family. Grandfather would do anything she said. They were devoted to each other. Watch.

(Rose leaves her two sons and approaches John & Ray.)

ROSE—John, dear, why don't you go take your seat.

JOHN—Yes, dear. (To Ray) Remember what I said, now.

RAY—Right, Papa, I won't forget.

(As John goes to the front row and sits, Rose looks at her son Ray with a very hard stare. He starts fidgeting with his tie again, clearly nervous at her attitude.)

ROSE—Your father is the kindest, sweetest man in the world. But he certainly isn't the smartest when it comes to these things.

RAY—What things, Mama? What are you talking about?

ROSE—That poor sweet man just gave you his little love and marriage speech, didn't he?

RAY—So?

ROSE—You can fool your father, Raymond Fortier, but don't you ever think you can do the same to me. I know all about your wild carousing and playboy ways.

RAY—Mama! Not so damn loud!

(Ray, takes her arm and pulls her stage front, looking back to see if anyone else heard her words.)

RAY—Mom, those days are all over. Honest! I love Winnie. I really do!

ROSE—As well you should, young man. I've gotten to know and love that girl over the past few months. She may not be the French girl I'd hoped you would find, but she has a big heart and there is no mistaking that. She's special, Raymond. Do you understand me?

(Ray throws his arms up in the air.)

RAY—Geez-Louise, Mama, this isn't the time for this! Ease up on me.

(Rose reaches up and grabs his tie, pulling his face down to her.)

ROSE—Very well, Raymond. But remember this. I don't know why, but I truly believe that girl loves you, for all your faults and I will not let her be hurt by that love.

RAY—Mama, please!

ROSE—Shut your mouth and listen, just once in your life. You will be a good husband to Winnifred and

you will be a good father to my grandchildren or
you will one day have to deal with me, young man.
Don't you ever forget that! God may forgive all
things, you just remember this, a mother does not.

RAY—I will, Mama. I promise. Now let go, please.

VALERIE—Did he keep his promise?

RON—Yes, very much so. Uncle Ray and Aunt Winnie
had a long and loving life together. They had five
children and lots of beautiful grandchildren and
great-grandchildren. They retired to Florida after
the kids had grown up and moved out. Recently they
celebrated their 60th wedding anniversary.

(Rose releases Ray's tie and then spends a few
seconds getting it straight.)

ROSE—Give me a kiss now and go get ready to greet
your bride.

(Ray hugs Rose and kisses her on the cheek.)

RAY—I love you, Mama.

ROSE—I know. God bless you and this day. Now shoo!

(Rose goes to join her husband, while Ray goes
over to stand in front of the altar and begins
conversing with the Priest.)

(At stage left, the two ushers, George & Richard
are seating people now coming in at a steady clip.
George is average height and very handsome, while
Richard is short. As George returns from having
seated two old ladies, he stands by the row where

Gaby and Cecile are sitting, his back to them. Both girls put their heads together to whisper.)

GABY—Cecile, who is he?

CECILE—I believe he and the other usher are the groom's brothers. I don't know what their names are.

GABY—God, he's so handsome. He's the most beautiful man I've ever seen.

CECILE—I know. He looks just like Ray Milland.

GABY—Why, you're right, Cil. He does look a lot like him.

VALERIE—Ray who?

RON—Milland. Ray Milland. He was a very handsome movie star back in the late thirties and early forties. Mostly romantic comedies. He eventually won an Oscar for playing an alcoholic writer in the film; THE LOST WEEK-END.

VALERIE—Really. And your father looked like him?

RON—Oh, yeah. Dad was twenty-one here and he was the spitting image of Ray Milland. They could have been twins. Now let's hush up and get on with the play.

(Gaby suddenly grabs Cecile by the arm.)

GABY—Golly, Cil! What if it is Ray Milland!

CECILE—Oh, for heaven's sake, Gaby. I told you, he's one of the Fortier brothers. I mean, look at him.

Does he act like a movie star?

(At this point a middle-age couple enters from stage left and George greets them nervously.)

GEORGE—Ah...ah...are you here with the groom or bride's family?

WOMAN—Winnifred is our niece.

GEORGE—Ah...very good. May I escort you to a pew?

(George offers his arm the woman graciously accepts.)

WOMAN—Thank you, young man.

(They start down the aisle, the husband following.)

WOMAN—Are you related to the groom?

GEORGE—Yes, ma'am. I'm his brother, George.

CECILE—See, I told you he was one of the brothers.

(Gaby still hasn't taken her eyes off George all the while he has seated the couple and is returning to his spot by the entrance.)

GABY—Oh, Cil. He's even dreamier than Ray Milland. He's for real.

(As Richard joins George, the music to the wedding march is heard.)

RICHARD—Well, that's our cue, George.

GEORGE—Right. Time for Ray to bite the dust.

(Chuckling softly, they walk to the front to take their places behind the Ray.)

(Everyone in the church rises as two young flower girls enter from stage left, leading the procession. Behind them come two maids of honor and then the lovely bride herself.)

CECILE—(Whispering to Gaby.)

She's so beautiful.

GABY—Oh, Cil, she must be so happy.

(As the bride reaches the altar, the lights at center fade away and those at the front go up to once more reveal Ron & Valerie.)

VALERIE (Looking to the now darkened and empty stage behind her.)

That's it? That's all there was to their first meeting?

RON—Now, remember dear, I said it wasn't an actual meeting but only the first time Mom set eyes on Dad. Sure, the writer in me thought of beefing it up a little. You know, show Mom and Aunt Cil sneaking into the reception and then having Dad see them.

VALERIE—Right. He could have brought them each a piece of the wedding cake or something.

RON—Then Mom would have clutched her folded hands over her heart as he walked away and proclaimed he was the man she was going to marry some day.

VALERIE—How romantic.

RON—And stupid.

VALERIE—Amen. Thanks for sparing us.

RON—It wasn't easy. Anyhow, that's more or less how Mom remembers it.

VALERIE—And your father?

RON—Dad says he didn't see her. He was too busy with being an usher and all. Besides, she was only a thirteen-year-old girl. There really wasn't any reason for him to notice her.

VALERIE—Okay. I'll buy that. So come on. Tell us the rest. When did they really meet for the first time?

RON—Four years later. But that is the theme of Act Two. Shouldn't we give the audience some kind of break here?

VALERIE—I don't think that's necessary. Act One was very short. Let's move on and we'll let them have an intermission before Act Three. How's that?

RON—Works for me. All right, on to Act Two.

(Ron turns waving his arm toward center stage and the lights there brighten while those over stage front once again dim.)

SANFORD, ME. CIRCA EARLY 1940S

ACT TWO

RON—By the fall of 1941 the drums of war were echoing across most of the globe. Hitler had launched his insane invasion of Russia and the Japanese were planning their attack on Pearl Harbor. My father had just completed two years in the New Hampshire National Guard. His enlistment ended, he came home. Army life wasn't for him. He hated taking orders all the time.

(Lights fade and stage is dark again.)

RON - At the same time, in good old Sanford, things were jumping!

(Music starts up. It is loud dancing music. Lights go up on center stage to reveal a large number of young people dancing the jitter-bug. Behind them on a raised platform is a band and an emcee standing before a microphone. A woman is standing next to the emcee and they are both whispering to each other while watching the dancing couples. At the center of the group of dancers is a brunette with long brown hair and she is dancing with a tall, skinny young man with short hair and wearing a brightly colored sweater. This is seventeen-year-old Gabrielle Richer and her older brother, Gene. The music finally stops and the couples all applaud loudly. The emcee thanks the band and then addresses the audience over the mike.)

EMCEE—Thank you, thank you. Aren't they a great band?

(The dancers cheer again.)

EMCEE—All right, we have the winners of our jitterbug contest. The judges have voted and their decision was unanimous. The winning couple is this fellow here with the sweater and his lovely partner.

(Gaby puts a hand over her mouth to stifle a scream and jumps into Gene's arms as the other couples applaud them.)

GABY—We won! I don't believe it, we won!

GENE—I know, Gaby! I told you we had a chance.

(The emcee jumps off the stage and approaches them, pulling an envelope out of his pocket.)

EMCEE—Congratulations, you two. Can I have your names, please?

GENE—I'm Gene Richer and this is my sister, Gaby.

VALERIE—That's your mother!

RON—Yes. She had turned seventeen November first of that year. She had grown into a lovely young woman.

EMCEE—Your sister. I see. No wonder you two dance so well together. I'll bet you practice a lot.

GABY—Every chance we get. Gene is a great dancer and he taught me all the right steps. I just love dancing.

EMCEE—Well, that's very clear to see, Miss Richer. And all that practice has paid off for you tonight.

(The emcee hands Gaby the envelope.)

EMCEE—Here is your prize of fifty dollars, compliments of the management here at the Algonquin Ballroom. Congratulation again.

GENE (Shaking hands with the emcee.)—Gosh, thanks. This is terrific.

GABY (Grabbing Gene's arm excitedly.)—Fifty dollars! Wow! Oh, Gene, that means we each get twenty-five dollars! All to ourselves.

(The emcee hops back to the stage and signals to the band to start another number.)

EMCEE—Okay, kids, lets keep those happy feet moving! The night is still young.

(The band starts up another fast tune and Gaby & Gene join their friends dancing again. The lights slowly fade out and the music dies out.)

VALERIE—Your mother was a really good dancer.

RON—She still is. It was her favorite thing to do. Uncle Gene was her partner and this was one of many dance contests they won while growing up in Sanford.

VALERIE—Did she have any boyfriends? I mean with her looks, she must have had to fight them off with a baseball bat.

RON—Oh, yeah. There were lots of them. The one she remembers most often was a guy named Moe. His father was the barber in town.

(The lights go up at stage right, where Gaby and a

young man, Moe Bouchard, are walking toward stage left, each of them wearing heavy winter clothes, with ice skates in their hands.)

MOE—Boy, Gaby, you sure know how to ice skate well. You're better than anyone on the pond.

GABY—Why, thank you, Moe. I think it's because of all the dancing I do. I seem to have a natural sense of balance.

MOE—It shows.

GABY—You're not so bad yourself, you know.

MOE—Aw, I'm fair most of the time. Thing is, Gaby, when I'm with you, I just naturally seem to do it better. You kind of inspire me.

GABY—I do?

MOE—Uh-huh. I just want to do things right so that you'll think highly of me.

GABY—I do already, Moe. It's not too many boys who could go to high school, play sports and still find time to work in a barbershop.

MOE—All I really do is just clean up and watch Dad. Although I do want to go to barber college when I graduate.

GABY—Heck, just going to high school would be enough for me. Sometimes I get so mad about not being able to go, I just want to sit down and cry. It's just not fair.

MOE—It's not your fault; your family couldn't afford it, Gaby. What with all your brothers and sisters, I think it's very admirable of you to go to work and help out like you do.

GABY—You do?

MOE—Uh-huh. In fact, I think you're lots smarter than most of those girls at the school. All they ever do is sit around fixing their make up and giggling to each other all day. Why, not one of them could hold a candle to you in the brains department.

(As they reach the left end of the stage, an elderly woman appears as if coming out of a door. She is Dorilla Richer, Gaby's mother.)

GABY—That's really nice of you to say that, Moe. Oh, hi, Mama.

MOE—Hello, Mrs. Richer.

DORILLA—Hello, Maurice. Did you have fun ice-skating?

GABY—Oh, Mama, it seems half the town was at the pond. Some men from the Fire Station built a big bonfire and it lit up the entire park. It was beautiful.

DORILLA—Well, that certainly sounds nice. Come on inside out of this cold. I made you both some nice hot chocolate to take the chill off.

MOE—That's swell, Mrs. Richer. I could sure use...

(A young man comes running onto the stage from the right curtain and yells when he sees the others. He is Billy Maddix, a neighbor.)

BILLY—Hey, everybody, did you hear the big news yet!

GABY—Why, Billy Maddix, what's got you so excited?

BILLY—We just heard it on the radio not five minutes ago!

MOE—Heard what?

BILLY—That the Japanese bombed Peal Harbor this morning!

DORILLA—Pearl what?

BILLY—Pearl Harbor. It's our navy base in Hawaii. My father says this is it for sure. We're going to war!

(Billy slaps Moe on the shoulder and starts to dash off.)

BILLY—I'm going around telling the gang.

MOE—Wait up! I'll go with you. Gaby, I'll see you tomorrow, okay?

GABY—Okay. See you tomorrow.

MOE—Goodnight, Mrs. Richer.

(Moe runs off stage where Billy exited.)

DORILLA—Goodnight, Moe. My goodness, this is awful.

I wonder if it's still on the radio. Come on, Gaby. Let's go inside. We have to tell Papa about this.

GABY—(Hugs herself and shivers.) Yes, Mama. All right. Suddenly, I feel a lot colder.

(Mrs. Richer goes over and wraps an arm around her daughter and together they exit stage left and the lights dim again.)

(Lights rise over Ron & Val.)

VALERIE—Wow, so that was it. The beginning of World War Two for America. It must have been frightening for them.

RON—It was, but for the most part, initially people just went about their normal routines. While the President and the government were mobilizing in Washington, average Americans went about their own affairs. Until the war reached them personally, there was nothing else to be done.

(The lights dim over Ron & Valerie and go up over rear stage right, where we see George & Richard. George is sitting on a chair reading a magazine, while Richard is putting on a tie.)

RON—It is now three months later. March of 1942. Dad is twenty-five years old.

RICHARD—So, how long do think it will be before the draft boards get around to us?

GEORGE—I don't know. I thought you were going to enlist?

RICHARD—I am. I was just curious, that's all. I mean, aren't you even a bit worried that they are going to come after you again?

GEORGE (Putting down his magazine and looking up at Richard)—I suppose. But I knew it was going to happen sooner or later. I just sort of wished it would have been a lot later.

(Rose Fortier enters stage right, wiping her hands in her apron. Richard goes right up to her immediately.)

RICHARD—Is my tie straight, Mama?

(Rose inspects the knot and does a little tugging on it.)

ROSE—There. You look very handsome tonight, Richard. You'll have to fight off all those Sanford girls at the dance.

RICHARD (Giving Rose and hug and kiss.)—Thanks, Mama. But none of them will be as pretty as you.

ROSE—Go on, now. Don't be trying that sweet talk on me.

(Rose turns to George, who has gone back to reading.)

ROSE—So, what about you, George? Aren't you going to the dance?

GEORGE—Naw, I thought I'd just stay home and listen to the radio with you and Papa and maybe do a little reading.

ROSE—You aren't going to meet any nice young girls that way.

RICHARD—That's what I told him, Mama. But he's just being an old stick-in-the-mud.

(Rose steps over to George and closes his book again. She reaches out and touches his face.)

ROSE—What is it, dear? Don't you want to meet a nice girl and settle down some day?

GEORGE—Sure, I do Mama. I just don't like dances. That's all.

RICHARD—That's true. He's got two left feet.

ROSE—You hush, Richard. Being a good dancer isn't everything!

GEORGE—At a dance it is. I just feel foolish when I hold a girl and then start tripping all over the place.

ROSE—Listen to me, George Fortier and listen good. Girls go to dances just for the same reasons boys do. And that isn't to dance. The dancing is just a way to meet. So what if you can't dance like Fred Astaire? God knows, your father is the clumsiest gorilla in the world when it comes to dancing. But I didn't let that put me off when we first met.

RICHARD—You married Papa because you loved him. Right, Mama?

ROSE—Yes I did. And I fell in love with him because he was a good and kind man with a beautiful smile and a heart to match. The same qualities all my boys have inherited to one degree or another.

(Rose looks down at George.)

ROSE—You, dear, got his good looks and dazzling smile. Trust me, George. No girls in their right minds will worry about your dancing when you take them in your arms. They'll just see that smile and it will sweep them away every time.

GEORGE (Getting up.)—All right, you talked me into it. I'll go to the bloody dance.

ROSE—That's my boy. Now give me a kiss and go put on your good clothes.

(George kisses Rose.)

GEORGE—Thanks, Mama.

(Lights dim over them. Lights come up over the entire stage again to show the Algonquin dance hall. The band and familiar emcee are there, while young people dance to happily jitterbug music. The difference now is that several of the boys are in service uniforms. Gaby is at stage left dancing with a boy.)

(George, Richard and another young man enter stage right. They stand there looking at the couples on the dance floor and the girls standing to stage left. The other man is Henry.)

RICHARD—Wow, this place is really jumping tonight.

HENRY (Points to where Gaby is dancing.)—Hey, check

out that little number over there. The one with the long brown hair. Man, oh, man, is she a real doll or what?

RICHARD—Whoa, tiger. We just got here.

HENRY—Waiting is for suckers. You know what they say about the early bird and the worm.

(The music stops and Henry immediately pushes his way through the crowds to reach Gaby and her partner.)

HENRY—Say, beautiful, can I have the next dance?

(Gaby looks at Henry surprised, then over at her partner, who only smiles and pats Henry on the back before walking off.)

DANCE PARTNER—Be my guest, pal. Maybe you can keep up with her. Me, I need a rest.

(The band starts to play another fast jitterbug and Henry and Gaby begin to dance.)

RICHARD—Boy, do you believe that guy?

GEORGE—I don't blame him, Dick. She's a knockout.

RICHARD—So, why don't you go ask her to dance?

GEORGE—I think I will. But first I need a beer. Is there a bar in this place?

RICHARD—Yeah, it's in the basement. Come on, I'll show you.

(George and Richard exit stage right and the lights dim over the stage. but the music continues playing. Lights go up over Ron and Valerie.)

VALERIE—"I need a beer." Sheesh, your father wasn't exactly what you would call the romantic type, was he?

RON—No. Thing is, he was extremely shy and felt awkward about how to approach her. So he went downstairs and had a few beers to bolster his courage.

VALERIE—That's funny. He didn't get drunk, did he?

RON—Oh, no. He only had two beers. An hour later he was back upstairs and ready to try his luck.

(Lights dim over Ron & Valerie and once again light up the dance floor. George is seen at stage right, fidgeting nervously from one foot to another, wringing his hands and watching the dancers. Gaby is now dancing with yet another boy. Henry is on the dance floor with a different partner, as is Richard. The music stops and couples walk off the floor. Gaby walks to the stage left to join the girls there...her sister Cecile is there also—this being an older actress playing the part.)

CECILE—(Nodding her head towards George.) I think you've got an admirer over there.

GABY—I know. I saw him come in about an hour ago.

(The band starts playing a slow song and George starts across the floor towards Gaby.)

CECILE—Don't look now, but here he comes.

(Gaby grabs at Cecile's hands nervously.)

GABY—Do I look all right? My hair, my lipstick? I'm not smudged or anything?

CECILE—Relax. You look great.

(George stops behind Gaby.)

GEORGE—Excuse me, Miss.

(Gaby turns around, brushing a strand off hair off her forehead.)

GABY—Yes?

GEORGE—May I...ah...would you like to dance?

GABY—I'd loved to.

(George extends his hand and she takes it. Together they walk to the center front of the stage and he takes her in his arms and they start slow dancing. Others couples come out to dance behind them.)

GABY—Are you nervous?

GEORGE—A little. Why? Is it noticeable?

GABY—Your body. It's so tight.

GEORGE—I'm sorry. I'm just not use to this.

GABY—What? Dancing?

GEORGE—Uh, huh. I'm afraid I'm not very good at it.

GABY—I see. I think the problem is you're trying too hard, that's all. The trick to dancing is just to enjoy yourself and have fun.

GEORGE—Well, you should know. I've been watching you dance and you're terrific.

GABY—Thank you.

(She looks up at him intently.) Say, you're a Fortier from Somersworth, aren't you?

GEORGE—(surprised) Right! How did you know that? Have we ever met before?

GABY—No. At least not formally. I remember seeing you at your brother's wedding a few years ago. The one who married Winnie Sharpe.

GEORGE—You were there? Strange. I don't remember seeing you there.

GABY—Well, I wasn't really a guest or anything. My sister and I just slipped into the back row at St. Ignatius's to watch the wedding. So, how are they doing?

GEORGE—Who? Ray and Winnie?

GABY—Uh-huh. Are they happy being married?

GEORGE—I think so. They have two kids now. A boy and girl and a third one on the way.

GABY—Wow! They sure didn't waste any time starting

a family, did they? I think that's wonderful.

GEORGE—You approve of families.

GABY—Of course. I'm one of eight myself. Oh, forgive me. My name is Gabrielle Richer. Everyone just calls me Gaby.

GEORGE—Hi, Gaby Richer. My name is George.

GABY—Hello, George Fortier. It's nice to meet you at last.

GEORGE—Likewise, Miss Richer...ah..Gaby. The pleasure is all mine.

(The dance comes to an end and they release each other.)

GABY—There. That wasn't so bad, was it?

GEORGE—Not at all. Thank you.

(The band starts to do another jitterbug and George makes a disapproving face.)

GEORGE—Well, that's it for me. This fast stuff is way out of my league.

(A young man seeing them just stand there, approaches Gaby.)

YOUNG MAN—Hey, Gaby! Let's cut up the rug!

(Gaby looks at the young man, then back to George and shakes her head negatively.)

GABY—Sorry, Dave. I'm going to sit this one out.

(The young man rushes past to find another partner among the group of girls at stage left.)

GEORGE—Would you like to go to the lobby and get a coke?

GABY—A cold drink sounds perfect right about now.

(With George leading the way, they walk around the dancers to stage right. Lights go off on dancers who now exit stage. At stage right a table is set up where a girl is selling sodas.)

GEORGE—Two cokes, please.

(The girl goes to a box/freezer and pulls out the two bottles. She puts them on the table near a bottle opener.)

GIRL—Twenty-cents.

(George hands her the two dimes.)

GEORGE—Thanks.

(George takes the opener and pops the cap off the first bottle and hands it to Gaby and then opens his own. They walk to center stage front which is now the dance hall lobby.)

GABY—Thank you. (She takes a small sip.) Ah. I was getting really hot out there.

GEORGE—I would never have guessed. You never seem to get tired.

GABY—Dancing is my favorite thing in the whole world. I just love it. My friends and I come here every chance we get. My brother, Jean, and I have even won several dance contests here.

GEORGE—That's great. Good for you. Maybe you should become a professional.

GABY—Ha. Now there's an idea.

GEORGE—I'm serious. I bet you could do it.

GABY—Oh, maybe. But it's just not practical. I mean, where would I start? Sanford, Maine isn't exactly the entertainment capitol of the world. Besides, I have my job to consider and my responsibilities at home.

GEORGE—Wouldn't your parents support you?

GABY—My mother would. But Papa would have a fit for sure. He's from the old school. You know, kids stay home and help support the family until it's time for them to get married and start their own families. Especially the girls.

GEORGE—Sounds familiar, all right. Although all we have in my family are boys. Still, if it was something you really wanted to do, I would think you'd have a right to decide for yourself. It's your life, after all.

GABY—Perhaps. Still, I love dancing because it is just fun to do. Maybe if it became a full time job I wouldn't feel the same way about it. You know, having to do something is a whole lot different than doing it because you just want to.

GEORGE—That's pretty smart. Not many people would figure that out.

(From stage left Cecile enters behind them.)

CECILE—Gaby. It's almost twelve. We have to go.

GEORGE—But I thought the dance went to one?

GABY—It does, but Mama says we have to be home by twelve.

GEORGE—Oh. Well, can I give you girls a ride home?

GABY—Sorry. That's against the rules too. It's okay. We only live a few blocks down the street. It's a five-minute walk, is all.

(They stand there just looking at each other until Cecile nudges Gaby's elbow.)

CECILE—C'mon!

GABY—I have to go. It's been very nice meeting you.

(She extends her hand and he takes it.)

GEORGE—Ah...yes, it has. Very much. I hope I'll get to see you again sometime?

GABY—That's easy enough. We're here most every week. Bye!

(Gaby dashes off stage right with Cecile, waving back. George waves farewell.)

GEORGE—Good-bye.

(He stands there just watching them leave. Then turns to face stage front with a lost, dreamy look on his face. Behind him Richard and Henry come up.)

RICHARD—Nice going, George. Looks like you made a hit with her.

HENRY—If you don't mind be called a cradle-snatcher.

GEORGE—What the hell do mean you by that, Henry?

HENRY—How old do you think that little cutie is, Fortier?

GEORGE—I don't know. Twenty?

(Henry folds his arms over his chest looking very smug.)

GEORGE—Nineteen?

HENRY—Try seventeen, Casanova.

GEORGE—Seventeen? You're kidding!

RICHARD—How do you know old she is, anyway?

HENRY—Because I asked, that's how. When we were dancing, I thought she looked familiar. I know her older brother, Jean Richer. So, while making conversation, I just asked and she told me. Why do you think I left her alone?

GEORGE—What are you saying?

HENRY—Look, she may have been the best-looking girl here but, hell's bells, she barely legal. No, sirree.

Seventeen is way too young for my taste. Now, you, on the other hand. If you really like that young stuff...

(Henry starts to put his arms around George's shoulders only to have George push him away.)

GEORGE—Knock it off, Henry.

HENRY—Okay, okay! I was only kidding. It ain't as if she was something special or something, right? You only just danced with her once, right.

GEORGE—Right.

RICHARD (To Henry.)—Leave him alone, will ya!

(George turns to Richard.)

GEORGE—Are you ready to get out of here?

RICHARD—I suppose.

GEORGE—Then let's go, okay?

RICHARD—Okay, okay! Whatever you say.

(George exits stage right with Richard & Henry following behind. Richard gives Henry a real hateful look, whereas Henry throws up his hands in the air to show to total befuddlement at George's sudden moody behavior. They exit. Lights dim out.)

(Lights up on left back side. Mrs. Richer sitting in a rocking chair, knitting. Donat Richer (a middle-aged man with a pot-belly, smoking a cigar) is at a table playing checkers with his son Gene. Cecile and Gaby enter stage left.)

GABY—Hi Mama, Papa.

DORILLA—How was the dance?

CECILE (Animated as she takes off her jacket and tosses it on an empty chair.)—Gaby made a new conquest tonight, Mama. A fellah from Somersworth.

DORILLA—Really. Is that true, Gaby? And Cecile, hang your coat in the closet. We don't live in a barn.

GABY (Having removed her own coat, hands it to Cecile, who takes both of them to backstage area out of sight.)—Oh, Mama. I just danced with him once. That's all. Cil is just making a big deal out of it, that's all.

CECILE (returning from off-stage)—I am not. He's a Fortier from Somersworth, Mama. His brother is the one who married Winnifred Sharpe a few years ago. Are there any more cookies in the kitchen?

(Before anyone can answer, Cecile exits stage back center.)

DORILLA—Just how old is this young man?

Gene—(Finally looking up from his game after taking one of his father's pieces.)—Hey, what's Moe going to say when he finds out you're playing around on him?

GABY—That's not true and you know it! Moe and I are just friends. Period. We're not steady or any such thing.

GENE—You could have fooled me. Are you sure Moe understands this the way you do?

DONAT—(He makes a move on the board and then nudges Gene.)—Pay attention to the game and stop yapping.

GENE—Right, Papa.

DORILLA—I asked how old he was, Gabrielle.

GABY—I don't know, Mama. What does that matter? He's so handsome.

(Cecile enters from where she disappeared; now holding a glass of milk in one hand and several cookies in the other.)

CECILE—I'll say. He looks just like Ray Milland.

DORILLA (Puts down her knitting.)—I'd say it's very important, young lady. Don't you agree Papa?

(Mr. Richer looks up at the mention of his name.)

DONAT—Huh? What? Whatever you say, dear.

DORILLA—We don't want Gaby dating older men, do we?

DONAT—Older? How much older?

GABY—I told you, I don't know how old he is.

DONAT—Is this fellow in the service?

GABY—I don't know, Papa!

DONAT—If he's so much older, he should be in the

service. Is there anything wrong with him? He's not one of them draft dodgers, is he?

(Gaby throws her hands up in the air.)

GABY—This is ridiculous.

DORILLA—Why? Because as your parents we are concerned for your well being? I consider that our obligation.

(Mr. Richer starts to make a move and Gene wags a finger at him.)

GENE—Are you sure you want to do that, Papa?

DONAT—Don't tell me how to play checkers, boy.

GABY—Mama, I only just met the man. We only danced one dance. That's all. Period. Cil is just blowing steam, having fun with you. Don't you see?

CECILE—Tell me you weren't excited about it? Go on, if you can.

GABY—It was just a dance.

CECILE—Yeah, right, and the Pope is just another priest.

DORILLA—Cecile Richer watch your mouth! The Pope is a holy man and will not be made fun of in my house.

CECILE—Sorry, Mama.

GABY—Look, everybody. George Fortier is a very nice

man and yes, he is handsome. But all I did was just dance with him one time. So can we just drop this? Please.

(Gene picks this moment to jump over his father's last few remaining pieces on the checkerboard.)

GENE—AHA! I win!

DONAT—SHIT!

DORILLA—PAPA!

(The lights dim. Lights then go up at stage front center where Gaby appears and is met by another girl her own age, entering from stage right. This new girl is Alice Wentworth.)

RON—The following Saturday night, Mom had to baby-sit and could not go to the dance. The next Sunday morning she ran into one of her friends on the street.)

GABY—Hi, Alice.

ALICE—Hi, Gaby. We missed you at the dance last night. They had a really swell band.

GABY—I had to baby sit for the Gagnons.

ALICE—There was a good-looking guy from Somersworth looking for you.

GABY—There was? Who was it?

ALICE—I don't know his name. Betty said it was the same guy who danced with you last week. He's tall, with wavy brown hair. A real looker.

GABY—Did he look like Ray Milland?

ALICE—Yes. Now that you mention it, he did. Anyway, he went all around the hall asking all the girls if you were going to come. He was really disappointed when you didn't show up.

GABY—How disappointed?

ALICE—He was crushed.

GABY—(she claps her hands) He was? That's great!

ALICE—Say, who is this guy, anyway?

GABY—Oh, just somebody I danced with.

(Gaby turns and skips away exiting, stage left.)

ALICE (To herself.)—Hmmm. He must be one hell of a dancer!

(She turns and exits stage right. Lights dim.)

(Lights go up over Ron & Val. They turn from the stage to look at the audience.)

RON—You women are vicious. Did you see how happy she was at his misfortune.

VALERIE—Now, now, don't go criticizing your mother for just being a teenage girl. She was just as captivated by your father as he was with her.

RON—True. She couldn't wait until the following

Saturday night to see if he would show up again.

(Ron turns and sweeps his arm toward center stage where the lights go up to reveal the dance hall again. Lights dim over him and Valerie. On the dance floor, Gaby is doing the jitterbug with Cecile. George and Richard enter stage right. George immediately spots Gaby and smiles.)

CECILE—Don't look now, but he just came in.

GABY—Who?

CECILE—George Fortier. He's over by the front door with his brother.

GABY—Has he seen us?

CECILE—I think so. He's looking this way and has this really stupid smile on his face. Wow, but you really did get to him, didn't you.

GABY—Cil. Stop exaggerating things.

(As the dance comes to an end, George makes his way to them. Richard walks off to find somebody to dance with. George comes up behind Gaby just as she turns.)

GABY—Oh. Hi, George.

GEORGE—Hi.

(The band starts to do another fast number. Gaby nudges Cecile with her elbow.)

CECILE—..Ah..I have to go to the washroom. (She

exits stage left.)

GABY—Want to dance?

GEORGE (Looks nervously as twisting couples around them.)

I'm not too good at this jitterbug stuff.

(Gaby reaches out and grabs his hand, pulling him into the crowd of dancers.)

GABY—It's easy. C'mon. I'll show you.

(They get lost in the crowd as the tempo of the music picks up. The lights dim out.)

(Music slowly fades away and lights come on an empty stage. George and Gaby, both wearing heavy coats enter stage right. They walking slowly side by side, Gaby limping slightly.)

GABY—Ooh!

GEORGE—It does hurt, doesn't it?

GABY—No, no. I just twisted it a little. Really.

GEORGE—I'm so sorry. I told you I was a lousy dancer.

GABY—It's all right, George. Really. You only stepped on it twice.

GEORGE—Well, at least let me help you here.

(He offers her his arm and Gaby smiles and takes it. They start walking again, slowly.)

GABY—All right. Thank you.

GEORGE—If I'm walking too fast, just say so.

GABY—No. This if fine. Really. You didn't have to walk me home. It's only down the street.

GEORGE—It the was the least I could do after nearly crippling you like that.

GABY—Will you stop worrying about my feet! I'm not some porcelain doll, you know! I don't break that easily.

GEORGE—I never thought you did.

GABY—Being brought up in a family of eight, you toughen up real fast. Especially with the awful depression and all.

GEORGE—Yeah, the country has really gone through some rough times. But it does look like things are turning around again.

GABY—Yes. Right into another war. Not exactly what I would call progress.

GEORGE—Maybe not, but it's not our fault about the war. The Japs did attack us first and as for Hitler, well, it's about time somebody went over there and stopped him for good.

GABY—But why does it have to be us? Didn't we already do that once? The nuns at school told us we fought in the last war so that there would never be any more wars. Yet here we are, already to go and fight another one. It's just not right.

GEORGE—Maybe not. I'm not sure why things worked out like they did. That's for the President and all the other bigwigs to figure out. I just think we have a responsibility to do this.

GABY—Does that mean you personally? Are you going to enlist?

GEORGE—No. I just finished two years with the National Guard last fall. They wanted to me re-enlist, but I was fed up with Army life and came home instead.

GABY—But won't you get drafted?

GEORGE—Most likely. I know it sounds crazy, but I just wanted to come home for a little while and now I'm more than glad I did.

GABY—Why is that?

GEORGE—I got to meet you.

(Gaby stops walking.)

GABY—Oh. Well, here we are. This is where I live.

GEORGE—Gaby...ah...can I ask you a personal question?

GABY—That depends on how personal.

GEORGE—How old are you?

GABY—I'm seventeen. Why? Does it make any difference?

GEORGE—Not to me.

GABY—I mean, it's a scientific fact that girls mature

lots faster than boys do.

GEORGE—Look, it's all right. It's just that...I...

GABY—Why? How old are you?

GEORGE—Me. Well...ah...I'm twenty-five.

GABY—Oh.

GEORGE—Damn, this is coming out all wrong. Look, Gaby, it's just that I don't want to get you into any kind of trouble. You know, with your folks or anything.

GABY—My parents trust me. Besides it's my decision who I see. Not theirs.

GEORGE—Then would you like to go out next Saturday? To a movie and then maybe get something to eat.

GABY—That sounds like fun. Okay. But we'll have to walk. I may be able to pick my own dates, but Mama is not going to bend on the car thing.

GEORGE—No problem. Besides, I like walking. I'll pick you up at seven. How's that?

GABY—Fine. I'll be looking forward to it.

GEORGE—Me to. Well, goodnight, Gaby.

GABY—Goodnight, George. Thanks for walking me home.

GEORGE—You're welcome.

(George turns and starts to walk off to stage right.

Gaby wrings her hands nervously then calls to him.)

GABY—George!

(He turns and she runs to him and kisses him fast and then runs off stage left.)

GABY—Bye.

(George stands there watching her leave, then touches his lips to feel the kiss. He smiles and starts skipping happily, hands clasped behind his back...he starts whistling happily and exits stage right.)

(Lights go up over Ron & Valerie.)

VALERIE—Your mother was certainly bold enough.

RON—No fooling.

VALERIE—Did they get much grief about their age difference?

RON—Oh, yes. Both families were concerned that this was an infatuation that would lead to pain and grief for both of them. Dad took a lot of teasing from his friends, whereas Mom had to constantly butt heads with my grandmother. Still they started dating on a regular basis, seeing each other at least once a week.

VALERIE—And they started to fall in love.

RON—They never got the chance. After only a few months, Uncle Sam stepped in and put a stop to their relationship.

(Ron & Val once more turn to face center stage as the lights dim out.)

RON—Or tried to.

(Lights go up as George & Gaby, walking side by side, enter stage right.)

GABY—That was the best Chinese food I ever had. I really made a pig of myself, didn't I?

GEORGE (Patting his own stomach.)—If you did, that makes two of us for sure. I love chop-suey. My mother makes it every now and then.

GABY—She must be a wonderful cook. Mama only knows French dishes she learned as a girl while growing up in Quebec. Sometimes we tease her about not cooking more American dishes.

GEORGE—And what does she say about that?

GABY—That she knows how to make hamburgers and hot dogs. That's enough American food for anybody.

GEORGE—Ha. I think she's right. So tell me. What did you think of THE THIEF OF BAGHDAD?

GABY—Oh, it was all right.

GEORGE—You didn't like it?

GABY—I just don't believe all that funny stuff. You know, the flying horses and genies and such. It was like a fairy tale for adults.

But I like seeing the cities and how the people

dressed. That was so beautiful. It's always been my secret dream to travel around the world someday. See all the wonders of far off places. That sounds silly, doesn't it?

GEORGE—Not at all. But I do hope you'll wait until this war is over before you go off and see the world. I'd imagine most of it is in a sad state these days.

GABY—Oh, you're putting me on. It really doesn't matter anyway because I'll never get to do it.

GEORGE—There you go being so darn practical again. Gosh, if you don't believe in your own dreams how do you ever expect any of them to come true?

GABY—Do you have any secret dreams?

GEORGE—Sure. Who doesn't?

(At this point they've reached stage left and Mrs. Richer enters wrapping a sweater about her soldiers.)

GABY—Mama?

DORILLA—So, how was the movie?

GABY—It was fun. Then we went for Chinese food at that little restaurant on Main Street.

DORILLA—I don't see what the appeal is of that food. What I've seen of it, it's mostly limpy vegetables and rice.

GEORGE—I guess you have to develop a taste for it.

DORILLA—(looking upwards at the sky)Perhaps. My, but it's a beautiful evening.

GEORGE—Yes, it is.

(Gaby is starting to fidget, wondering exactly what it is her mother is doing there.)

GABY—Ah, Mama. Is there something you wanted?

DORILLA—Yes, my dear. There is. I wanted to have a few words with George away from your father and the rest of the family.

GABY—About what?

DORILLA—If you'll be quiet for a second, I'll get on with it.

(She turns to George and clasps her hands together to stand a bit straighter before him.)

DORILLA—I would very much like to know what your intentions are towards Gabrielle.

GABY (Screams)—Mama! I can't believe you're doing this! I am so embarrassed!

DORILLA—I'm only doing what any good mother would do in such a situation.

GABY—Oh, God, this is so embarrassing. George, I'm so sorry. I had no idea she was going to do this.

GEORGE—It's all right, Gaby. I really respect what your mother is doing.

GABY—You do?

DORILLA—Thank you, George. But you still have not answered my question.

GEORGE—Well, I guess the truth is, my intentions, as of today, are not important anymore.

DORILLA—I do not understand you?

(George reaches into his coat pocket and pulls out a white envelope. He holds it up to Mrs. Richer.)

GEORGE—This came in the mail this morning. It's my draft notice. I have to report to Boston in a week for shipment to Ft. Dix in New Jersey.

GABY—Oh, George. Why didn't you tell me sooner?

GEORGE—I didn't want to spoil our date. I figured I'd wait until after we got back from the movie. So you see, Mrs. Richer, I'm leaving and you won't have to worry about my intentions after all.

DORILLA—Forgive me, George. I would not have wished this on any young man. I will keep you in our prayers and ask the Blessed Virgin to keep you safe from harm until the war is over.

GEORGE—Thank you, Mrs. Richer. I appreciate that.

(Mrs. Richer turns and kisses Gaby.)

DORILLA—Good night, dear. Don't stay up too late. It's still cool out.

GABY—I won't, Mama. Good night.

(Mrs. Richer exits stage left and Gaby leads George to a porch bench where they sit side by side.)

GABY—Oh, George, I don't know what to say.

GEORGE—Hey, don't worry. It's not like I wasn't expecting it. And besides, with my guard experience, at least I won't have to do basic training over. They're just going to process me in Dix and then send me to some artillery outfit somewhere else.

GABY—Do you think you'll go to Europe?

GEORGE—There or the South Pacific. There's no way of telling. When you're in the Army you just go where they send you.

GABY—Will I see you again before you leave?

GEORGE—Sure. I'll try to get over here next Saturday. I leave Sunday morning.

GABY—You'll have to send me your address so that I can write to you.

GEORGE—Okay. I'd, like that. But you know...there is something we should get straight.

GABY—What?

GEORGE—As much as I've liked being with you these past few weeks and all, I don't want you thinking this is more that what it is.

GABY—What are you saying?

GEORGE—That it's not like we were going steady or

anything. Look, Gaby, I just don't know how long I'm going to be gone. It could be years.

GABY—And you don't want me to wait for you. Is that what you're trying to say?

GEORGE—Yeah, right. I don't expect you to just sit around on my account. That would be crazy. I know how much you love going out and dancing. No way do I want you give all that up.

GABY—I suppose you're right. You could meet other girls wherever you're stationed too.

GEORGE—Look, Gaby, I just don't want us to make promises that are impossible to keep. That seems wrong to me. Let's just let it go that we're friends and we'll just write to each other.

GABY—That sounds perfectly logical. Still, I am going to miss you when you go.

GEORGE—Me, too. These past few weeks with you have been wonderful, Gaby. You're really a very special girl.

(Gaby puts her arms around his neck.)

GABY—Then how about giving this special girl a kiss goodnight.

(They kiss.)

GABY—You know, Mr. Fortier, for a so-so dancer, you are one terrific kisser.

(They kiss again and the lights dim out as scene ends.)

(Lights go up over Ron and Valerie and they again turn to front.)

VALERIE—And so your father went off to war just as he and your mother were getting to know each other.

RON—That's how it happened.

VALERIE—Did he really tell her to go and date other guys?

RON—Yes. Although he was really taken with her, Dad honestly didn't think a seventeen year girl, especially a pretty one like Mom, could ever stay faithful to someone who would be gone for a long time. He more or less figured she would write him a few letters and eventually even they would stop.

VALERIE—And your mother. How did she feel about his leaving?

RON—Pretty much the same. She liked him a great deal and they had hit if off right from the start. But she never thought their relationship would continue after he shipped out. Boy, was she in for a surprise.

VALERIE—This is where they eventually come to fall in love through their letters, isn't it?

RON—Pretty much. But that's act three and we did promise these good people an intermission before that. So what do you say we all take a fifteen minute breather to stretch our legs, maybe run out to the lobby to get a drink and then come back for the big finale.

VALERIE—Sounds good to me. (To the audience.) See you in fifteen minutes.

(Arm in arm, they exit to center stage and the curtains close.)

SOMERSWORTH, NEW HAMPSHIRE

ACT III

(Lights go up and curtain opens. Ron and Valerie enter stage left.)

RON—Welcome back. (To Valerie.) All set for Act Three?

VALERIE—Yes, I am. I suppose you're going to set the mood for us again.

RON—I'll do my best.

(They walk to stage left front and the lights over them fade.)

RON—By the time 1943 had rolled around the war was in high gear and a cold, all-pervading fear had gripped America. Hitler's mad invasion of Russia had failed miserably at the cost of thousands of lives on both sides. President Roosevelt and British Prime Minister Winston Churchill met in Casablanca to plot out their strategy for reclaiming Europe. They chose to invade Sicily first. Among the British soldiers who would fight in the Italian campaign was Winnie the Pooh's grown up Christopher Robin Milne.

Back home the U.S.Postal Service took on a very dramatic and unwanted role.

(A middle aged mailman enters center stage, while an elderly couple appears at stage right. The mailman walks to them and tips his hat, while handing the man an envelope from his pouch.)

MAILMAN—Good morning, Doctor Thompson. Mrs. Thompson.

DR.THOMPSON—Good day, Joe. What do you have for us?

MAILMAN—It's from the...War Department, sir.

MRS.THOMPSON (Grabbing her husband's arm.)—Oh, God, no!

(Dr. Thompson opens the letter and then squints at it. He hands it back to the mailman.)

DOCTOR THOMPSON—Would you read it, Joe? I don't have my glasses with me at the moment.

MAILMAN (Taking the letter.)—Sure, Doc. It's addressed to both of you. Doctor and Mrs. Arthur Thompson, of Sanford, Maine. Then it starts...We regret to inform...you...

(Mailman pauses and looks at the couple. Mrs. Thompson is crying. Doc nods for Mailman to continue.)

MAILMAN—...while engaged with enemy forces in the South Pacific, on March twenty-fifth, your son, Arthur W. Thompson was killed during action aboard the destroyer Lexington. Please know that you have the sympathies of the President and a grateful nation in this time of supreme sacrifice. Then it's signed by the Secretary of the Navy.

(Doc takes the letter back and slips it into his coat pocket. He and Mrs. Thompson, now sobbing in his arms, turn and exit stage right.)

MRS.THOMPSON—My baby. My baby.

(Mailman watches them walk off and then turns and

walks off in the opposite direction, head hung low, mumbling to himself.)

MAILMAN—He was a good kid. Played baseball with my boy, Harry. Had a terrific fast ball. Don't seem right, somehow. Dying so far away from home at such a young age. It's a damn shame. That's what it is, a damn shame.

(Mailman exits stage left. Lights fade out.)

RON—After Dad left for the Army, Mom was true to her words and began writing him, although at first her letters were infrequent because he kept getting moved around from base to base. Eventually he ended up in Los Angeles.

VALERIE—L.A. Really? How come there and not overseas?

RON—You have to remember, dear, after the attack on Pearl Harbor, Americans living on the west coast were convinced the Japanese would eventually cross the Pacific and attack them. There was a great deal of hysteria at the time and the military leaders decided to bolster our defenses there. My father, being an artillery man, was assigned to a gun battery positioned in the hills overlooking Hollywood.

VALERIE—Did he meet any movie stars while he was out there?

RON—Watch. You'll see.

(Lights go up over stage center. Enter Gaby and Moe from stage right. Gaby is holding a box of popcorn and eating from it.)

MOE—Boy, that newsreel about General MacArthur was grand. I'm sure he and his troops will kick those lousy Nips all the way back to Japan in no time flat.

GABY—I hope so. The war just seems to be dragging on and on. I'm so scared for my brothers. And Mama is beside herself with worry all the time.

MOE—Gosh, Gaby, I get so frustrated some times. I should have gone like all the guys in my class.

GABY—Moe, it's not your fault you have flat feet.

MOE—Maybe not, but every time we go to the dances or movies and I see all those guys in uniforms. I feel like some kind of yellow skunk. I do.

GABY—That's not true. Your work with the Red Cross and the Civil Defense is very important here. It's like the President said on his radio show last week, we have to keep up the Home Front war as well to support our men fighting overseas.

MOE—I suppose you're right. Thanks, Gaby. I can always count on you to lift my spirits whenever I get down.

GABY—Well, that's what friends are for, isn't it.

MOE—Is that all we are, Gaby? Just friends? I thought...had hoped, we were maybe something more?

GABY—I know, Moe. It's not that I am unaware of that but the truth is, I don't feel ready for anything else right now.

MOE—I see. Are you sweet on another guy? Is that it?

GABY—No. I'm not seeing anybody else. You know that.

MOE—Is it that soldier you've been writing to?

GABY—George Fortier? Moe, I told you, he's just a friend. Like you.

MOE—Then why do you always get so excited whenever he writes you?

GABY—I do not.

MOE—Yes, you do.

GABY—Well, maybe a little. But besides, he's stationed in Hollywood and seeing all those famous places for real. I find that terribly exciting. There's nothing wrong with that.

MOE—No, there isn't. I'm sorry. It's just that, well, I love you, Gaby.

GABY—Moe, please.

MOE—I always have and you know it. But you never seemed to care about that and...well...a guy just can't wait forever.

GABY—If I've hurt your feelings, I'm sorry, Moe. I've never allowed you think anything else.

MOE—You've always been straight with me, Gaby. I know that.

GABY—Good. I hope we can always be friends, Moe. But that's all I can give you. Don't be mad at me, please.

MOE—I could never be that. Look, it's late and I have to go. I'll see you later.

GABY—Goodnight, Moe.

(Moe turns and rushing, exits stage right. Gaby wrings her hands.)

GABY—Why does life have to be so complicated all the time?

(Gaby turns and starts to walk to stage left just as Cecile enters from there waving an envelope at her.)

CECILE—You got another letter from George. It just came this afternoon.

GABY—Thanks, Cil.

(Gaby tears opens the envelope and takes out the folded pages inside.)

CECILE—Come on, read it aloud. I want to know if he's met any of those movie stars yet.

GABY—Don't rush me. All right, here it goes.

Dear Gaby, how are you? I hope all is well with you and your family. Things are pretty quiet out here. Which I suppose is a good thing after the Zoot Suit Riots they had a month ago. You must have read about them in the papers. Seems a couple of

Mexicans, wearing those big, gaudy Zoot suits came into Los Angeles looking to pick up some girls and got into a fight with some soldiers. It got out of control and pretty soon all kinds of people were joining in the mayhem. By the time it was over, lots of storefronts had been smashed up pretty good and a few black boys were killed when the mob went after them for no good reason.

(Gaby stops reading and looks at Cecile.)

GABY—How can people be so cruel? To go crazy like that and hurt complete strangers.

CECILE—Just keep reading the letter. It's not for us to figure out why those soldiers went nuts.

GABY (Going back to the letter.)—Anyhow, the result was putting L.A. off limits to all military personal going on leave. Which is a really bad thing since a lot of us are out here for the very first time are now denied the chance to see the city.

GABY—I'm just glad this ruling doesn't apply to Hollywood itself because then what happened last Sunday would have been impossible. You see, I finally got to meet a real life movie star.

CECILE—Who was it? Who? Who?

GABY—I'm getting to it! Will you relax a little. Now where was I? Oh, yes, here it is. He goes on to say,

...having a day pass, I took the bus down to the Hollywood canteen and thought I would just hang around for a while. Maybe play some cards with some of the other guys and see if anybody famous came in.

(Lights over Gaby fade out and come up at stage left. There we see a small counter with a girl standing behind it. She has a list in her hand and is speaking into a microphone.)

GABY—Many of the local personalities have started coming to the canteen to pick up servicemen and bring them back to their homes for dinner. Sort of their way of being patriotic. Lots of stars are doing it. So when I got to the canteen I went to the hospitality desk and signed up. It was only about twenty minutes later when I heard my name being paged.

GIRL AT THE DESK—Will the following men please report to the courtesy desk. Corporal Armand Vachon and Private George Fortier.

(From back center stage George and another soldier, Cpl. Vachon appear.)

GIRL—You are Corporal Vachon and Private Fortier.

CPL VACHON—That's right, sweetheart. What's up?

GIRL—We just received a call from one of our most generous citizens asking if there were two hungry servicemen who would like to have dinner with his family. He's on his way now to pick you up.

GEORGE-Gee, who is it?

GIRL—I don't want to spoil your surprise, boys. He should be here any minute now.

CPL VACHON—This is rich. I wonder who it could be? Hey, maybe it's Bob Hope. I hear he does this sort of stuff all the time.

GEORGE—So does John Wayne. Hell, it could be anybody.

GIRL (Looking towards stage right as lights come up over entire stage.)—You don't have to guess anymore. Here he comes now.

(A small man with a white hat and a pipe in his mouth comes strolling onto the stage.)

CPL VACHON—Holy Moses! It's Bing Crosby himself!

CROSBY—Hi, Molly. Boys. How are you doing out here in Tinsel town? The folks here at the canteen showing you a good time?

GEORGE—Oh, sure, Mr. Crosby. Everybody here is swell. They really try to make a guy feel at home.

CROSBY—That's what I wanted to hear. Say, are you boys good and hungry? We have this turkey dinner waiting back home and need some really big appetites to do it justice.

CPL VACHON—Turkey! That's my favorite. Just lead the way, Mr. Crosby. We'll be right behind you.

CROSBY—Then let's go, boys. Don't want Mrs. Crosby wondering if I got lost on the way here.

(With Crosby in the lead, the others start walking to stage right just as a group of young girls enters there. They spot the boys.)

CROSBY—I left my automobile right out here on the corner.

GIRL IN LEAD—Oh, my God, girls! Look!

CROSBY—Oops! Seems like we've been spotted.

SECOND GIRL—It's him! It's really him!

CROSBY — Sorry about this boys. This sort of thing happens all the time.

(The girls rush across the stage as Crosby takes off his hat to brush his hair back...but the girls rush past him and surround George.)

LEAD GIRL—It's Ray Milland!

SECOND GIRL—Can I have your autograph, Mr.Milland.

(Lights fade out as scene ends. Go up at the front over Ron and Valerie.)

VALERIE—You made that up?

RON—No, I did not. Dad actually met Bing Crosby and went to his house for dinner exactly as I've shown.

VALERIE—And the mix-up with Ray Milland?

RON—It happened all the time once he got out to Hollywood. Dad was very uncomfortable about it after the first few times it happened. Much to the annoyance of his buddies. When they saw the girls falling all over him, they tried to persuade him to play along and say he was Ray Milland.

VALERIE—What did your father do?

RON—He refused hands down. My father was extremely

shy, and odd as it might sound, he did not like having all these girls throwing themselves at him.

VALERIE—A condition that would not have bothered you in the slightest.

RON—Hey, I'm only human. Not many men could have resisted that kind of good fortune. But it just wasn't in dad's nature.

VALERIE—So what happened? Did his pals leave him alone about it?

RON—They did stop suggesting he lie about his identity, but they didn't stop hanging around with him whenever he went into town. Nine out of ten times, girls would be attracted to him and his friends naturally tried to take advantage of the situation any way they could. Sort of using Dad like a chick magnet.

VALERIE—Did he tell all this to your mother in his letters?

RON—He did. Dad had done nothing to hide from her and my Mom found his shyness to be very appealing.

VALERIE—Most women would. So how long did his stay in California last?

RON—A little over a year. With the war in the South Pacific going well for the Allies, the likelihood of the enemy ever reaching our shores became more and more remote. Enough so that the Army decided it was time to transfer these valuable, and fresh, troops to the combat theater. Thus, in 1943 my father's unit was shipped to Philippines to protect newly built air strips on those islands recaptured by American forces.

(Ron turns to indicate the stage and the lights over them once again dim. Lights go up over stage left, where George is seen sitting on a bunk bet, with a pad of paper in hand. He is composing a letter. To the right of him, three other soldiers seated on the floor around a foot locker playing poker on its surface.)

GEORGE (Picking up his note pad, reads from it.)— Dear, Gaby. Well here I am in Guadalcanal. It is hot as hell here and you feel like a wet dishrag all the time. They warned us about not walking around without any skin covering as it is real easy to get sunburned here. We also have to take quinine pills once a day as to prevent malaria and God knows what else.

(Lights go up over right side where Gaby is seen sitting on her on bed, reading his letter.)

GEORGE—What I wouldn't give for a good old New England snow storm right now. Here it is October and you can't tell a thing. All the seasons are exactly the same here. Except...

GABY—...,that is, for the monsoon seasons which bring lots of rain. So much so, the guys who have been here a while, say that you can stand outdoors and take a shower in the warm rain. So how are things back home? Do the papers still carry all the news about the war and how we're doing out here? Most of the time we just sit around bored if we don't have duty. And that usually means digging sand bags. Lots and lots of sandbags. I have the blisters to prove it. As you know, our job is to protect the airfields from Jap bombers. So far I've only been through one air raid and it was over in a matter of minutes. They flew over, dropped some bombs that fell way off the mark into the jungles and then the all clear siren sounded and it was back to our tents. What a life. Mail from home still hasn't reached me yet and I hope it comes soon. This waiting is for the birds. Well, got to run. Take care, all my best, George.

(Gaby puts down the letter and picks up her own pad of paper and pen and starts writing.)

GABY—Dear George, it is difficult for me to read your letters with you so far away and try to imagine all the things you are going through. I guess none of us safe and sound at home will ever know all the sacrifices you are making.

GEORGE—(continues her letter) Except that we do miss you all so much. Downtown Sanford is so strange on week ends. When you go out, all you see are women, babies and old people. The absence of so many young men is clearly felt and just makes it all the more unreal. And it seems every day we hear of someone else who has died in the fighting.

The stars that people put in their front windows keep popping up all over. At mass last Sunday, Father Lenoix said we have to keep praying that God will end this horrible war soon and bring you all home again.

(George puts down her letter, picks up a notepad and starts to write his own back to her.)

GEORGE—Dear Gaby, I was very glad to hear about the winter carnival and how much fun you had skating there with your friends. The Japs hit us real hard last night. There must have been two dozen bombers trying to blow up the strip.

GABY—(continues reading his letter) We were up most of the night, shelling the skies trying to shoot them down. It is hard at times with the booming noise of the guns and the flashes to know if you do hit anything at all. A couple of the enemy planes managed to get through and dropped a few bombs along the edge of the runway. The Seabees have been working all day long to repair it so that our planes can get back into the air. One shell hit next to Battery B and bits of shrapnel hit the crew. Luckily no one was killed, but a nice guy named Walters, from Ohio, got a big chunk in his leg and was rushed to the base hospital. Word is he's got one of those million dollar wounds that will get him sent home.

GEORGE—(now reading Gaby's reply)Dearest George, I hope this box of Christmas goodies reaches you in one piece. Mama baked the cookies and Papa made the potato chips himself. The paperback novels and comic books are mostly westerns as I recall you saying those were your favorites. We showed everyone your pictures and the men in the family were very impressed by the ones of the gun batteries. One of the boys down the street wanted to know if the island girls were beautiful and whether or not they wear any clothes. Thank you so much for the beautiful birthday card and the pearl necklace. I wear it all the time. You must have paid a fortune for it. You shouldn't spend your money on me. You should put it away for when you get home. Do you get to read about the war in Europe? Everyone is saying that it is only a matter of time before we invade Europe and go after Hitler. In a newsreel at the movie house, they showed Princess Elizabeth working in a machine shop. She is eighteen and is a fully qualified mechanic. Isn't that incredible? A real-life princess working as a mechanic. Papa says she must charge an arm and a leg. Love and kisses, Gaby.

GABY—(reads one of George's letters) Dear Gaby, We were all thrilled to hear about D-Day over here. Looks like that General Eisenhower really knows what he's doing. Whereas we are still having to fight toe to toe with the Japs. Having to take every single island has become a real nightmare and we hear through the grapevine that casualties, especially among the marines, are very high.

On a lighter note, you remember that kid I told you about, Billy Ray Cougan, who comes from the Louisiana swamp country and goes around bare-footed all the time. Well, he's gone and built a still in the jungles near our camp and is selling moonshine whiskey to the sailors out on the ships anchored here. The C.O. got wind of it and called him on the carpet for it, ordering him to go out there and destroy it. Old Billy Ray just played dumb and told the Captain, if he could find the still, he could smash it himself.

Everyone knows those jungles are real dangerous, what with snakes and even some Jap snipers still on the loose. In the end the Captain let him go. Boy, was he ever mad. That's one thing about being in the army I have always appreciated and that is being able to meet and get to know so many guys

from all over the country. It is a real education
for me. Love, George.

GEORGE—(reading a letter from Gaby)June 20th. Dear
George, summer has arrived at long last and most
of southern Maine is in the middle of a very dry
heat wave. Enough so that the radio is full of
public service announcements from the Department
of Forestry warning everyone about the risks of
forest fires. Papa got so fed up with the heat the
other night; he packed us all up in his big truck
and drove us down to Old Orchard Beach. We got to
sit in the back and it was great. The park was wild
as ever with a lot of Canadians down for the season.
Cecile, Tanse and I ate so much junk, we were all
sick with stomach cramps most of the night. Mama
kept shaking her head and telling us to act our
ages. Well, politics are back in the news too with
the elections coming up in November. Everyone is
sure Governor Dewey hasn't got a chance in beating
President Roosevelt. Still it is fun to see all the
local rallies and meetings with the red, white and
blue stickers everywhere you look. Lets see, what
else is new. Oh, almost forgot. The Messier boy who
lives down the street is said to have polio. Mrs.
Messier's sister from Bangor is staying with the
family to help out. They say she's a nurse and has
been a real blessing to them, what with Mr. Messier
away in Europe with the Army and now this. God, it
is so sad how some people have to suffer more than
their share of grief in this life.

On a brighter note, fashions are changing pretty
fast thanks to the shortage of goods and materials.
Stockings are almost extinct and those you can
find at local stores are twice as much as last
year at this time. Some of the girls have started

painting thin black lines down their legs to give
the appearance they are wearing sheer hose. And
there is a lot more leg to see as the skirts have
started getting real short again. Cil and I can't
go down Main Street without the men in front of
the barber shop whistling as we go by. I'd swear
some of those dirty old men had never seen a pair
of legs in their entire lives. Still, it is fun to
imagine oneself being a pin-up model like Betty
Grable or Rita Hayworth. Say, do you have any of
those pictures in your foot locker?

Just curious. I mean, I don't mind if you do and
you really don't have to tell me if you don't want
to. Well, before I go and say something else totally
stupid, I'll quit for now. Please take care of
yourself. Love always, Gaby.

(George puts down the letter and picks up a photo
on the bunk beside his writing material. It is of
Gaby.)

GABY—(reading his reply) July 15. Dear Gaby, before
anything else, let me assure you I do not have any
pin-ups in my foot locker or anywhere else for that
matter. The only pictures I have there are of you
and they are all I need. Besides, your legs are ten
times shapelier than Betty Grable's and if I were
back home right now, I'd be whistling too. I have
a confession to make and I know you'll understand
what I'm saying here. When you first promised to
write me, I honestly thought you would stop after
a while. Now, here I am getting a letter from you
every single day and you will never truly know just
how much they mean to me. Sometimes, at night, I
lay awake on my bunk listening to the night noises
from the jungles and I get so scared about all this.

Where I am and what's going on out here. Sometimes it's enough to drive a guy nuts. But then I'll just read through some of your letters and they make everything okay again. Just to know you are there is all that matters. So, I guess what I'm saying is, I love you with all my heart and soul. George.

(Gaby holds the letter up and rereads the last line.)

GABY—I love you with all my heart and soul.

(She folds the letter and puts it over her heart.)

GABY—Oh, George. I love you too.

(Lights go up over Ron and Val.)

VALERIE—She actually wrote to him every single day?

RON—During his last year overseas, yes. He did likewise but sometime in the spring of 1945 his letters stopped coming.

(Lights dim over Ron and Val and George. They remain over Gaby now rushing to stage center. Joe, the mailman, enters stage left and they meet.)

MAILMAN—Good morning, Gaby. (He hands her a bunch of letters.) I'm sorry, dear. There's nothing from your fella.

GABY—Oh. I see. Thanks, anyway, Joe.

MAILMAN—Don't you fret now. Lots of reason why the mail gets held up during war time. Heck, it just might be sitting on some dock in San Francisco waiting to be sorted out.

GABY—You think so?

MAILMAN—Dear, in my sixteen years with the U.S. Postal Service, I've seen every kind of foul up there is. You just have to have faith. You'll see, it'll all be fine. Good day, now.

(Joe walks off and Gaby stands there holding the letters in her hands. Mrs. Richer enters stage left and seeing Gaby looking sad, stops in mid step.)

DORILLA—No letter from George?

GABY—No, Mama. Nothing and it's been over two weeks now! He's never gone this long without writing to me. Mama, I'm afraid. What if...he's...

(Gaby rushes into her mother's arms and begins to cry.)

DORILLA—There, there, my sweet one. You must be brave now.

GABY—But what if he's dead, Mama? I couldn't stand if anything happened to him, Mama! I couldn't!

DORILLA—Don't talk like that! We know nothing of the sort. Poor George could be just sick or hurt. Maybe he's being transferred to another island and that's why he has not been able to write you.

GABY—Oh, Mama. If anything ever happened to him, I'd die.

DORILLA (Pushes Gaby to arms length.)—He has come

to mean this much to you, has he?

GABY—Yes, Mama. I love him and he loves me. Oh, Mama, what am I going to do?

DORILLA—What good people of faith always do when they are afraid, you are going to pray to God and ask him to watch over your young man. And you will trust that He will you hear you. He always does.

(Mrs. Richer kisses Gaby on the forehead and exits stage right. Gaby clasps her hands together and slowly begins to pace back and forth, looking upward.)

GABY—(she crosses herself) Heavenly Father, I feel so ashamed coming to you like this when I know there must be thousands of other women doing the very same thing. Mothers and wives and sisters all praying to you to watch over their men folk just as I am doing right now. Still, I believe, like Mama says, that you hear all our prayers. Oh, God, please let George be all right and send your angels to watch over him for me. He is such a good and decent man and I love him so much. For the first time in my life, I have come to realize what is most important. It's not the dances and parties or any such goings on. All that amounts to zero if you don't have someone to love and who loves you. Nothing matters if you don't have someone special to share your hopes and dreams with. Oh, please, dear God in heaven, let him come home to me. Please.

(Gaby starts to exit stage right. Stops and looks up again.)

GABY—Thank you. Amen.

(Head bowed low, she exits and lights dim.)

(Lights go up at stage left where we see Gene and Donat Richer sitting together on the front porch playing checkers again this over a small card table. There is a radio playing on the small table behind them. From stage right comes Billy Maddix, only now he is in uniform and has his arm in a sling.)

BILLY -Good afternoon Mr. Richer, Gene.

DONAT — Hello Billy.

GENE — Hey, Billy.

BILLY — Can I play the winner?

DONAT — Sure thing. Won't take me long to finish this game.

GENE - (annoyed by the comment)

I ain't beat yet.

DONAT - (back to Billy)So how's the arm coming? Is it healing okay?

BILLY — Yes, sir. The doctors say I was lucky and that the bullet only tore up a little bit of muscle. With rest and exercise, it should be as good as new in time.

DONAT — That's good, Billy. A man today needs two strong arms to make his mark in this world. Hard work is what it's all about.

BILLY — Yes, sir. I guess you're right.

GENE — Did you really get the purple heart, Billy?

BILLY — Uh-huh. My dad keeps it on the mantel in the living room.

GENE — Geepers, I wish I were old enough to get in the war.

(Donat suddenly reaches out across the table and cuffs Gene across the side of the head, startling more than anything.)

GENE — YOWWW! Why'd you that for?

DONAT — Because, boy, sometimes too much courage is stupid!

(The music over the radio stops suddenly and a reporter's urgent voice comes across, getting the men's attention.)

VOICE OVER RADIO—Flash! We interrupt this program to bring a special announcement. Dateline, Warm Springs, Georgia. President Franklin Delano Roosevelt, while on vacation in Warm Springs, collapsed this afternoon while posing for a new portrait. He was pronounced dead at three-thirty-one this afternoon. I repeat, the President of the United States, Franklin Delano Roosevelt is dead at the age of sixty-three. We will continue to bring you more information on this sad occasion as we receive it here at the studio.

(As the music starts up again, Billy, shakes his head in disbelief.)

BILLY—Oh, God, no! Not now.

DONAT — He was a great man.

GENE — Gosh, Papa. What's going to happen to the country now? What will we do?

DONAT — What Roosevelt would have wanted us to do. We're going to win this war and bring our boys home. You mark my words, both of you. Now, more than ever, that's what we're going to do. We're going to win.

(Lights fade out. Lights go up as Joe the mailman enters stage left, carrying his mailbag and sorting through it as he walks along. Cecile enters stage right and on seeing him, rushes to meet him. He hands her one single letter.)

MAILMAN—Here it is, Cil. The one she's been waiting for.

CECILE—Oh, thank you, Joe. Thank you.

(Joe turns and exits stage left as Cecile turns to stage right and yells.)

CECILE—Gaby! You got a letter!

(Gaby enters running from stage right, followed slowly by her mother, who is wiping her hands on her apron.)

GABY—Is it from George? (She grabs the letter.)

CECILE—It's the same APO address but...

GABY (Looking mixed up as she studies the address.)—

It's not his handwriting! It's not from him!

DORILLA—There, there now. What's the matter?

(Gaby turns and shows her the letter.)

GABY—It's a letter from George's outfit addressed to me but it's not his handwriting. Mama, what does it mean?

DORILLA (Reaches out and grabs Gaby's arm.)Calm down and let us see. Look, it is not an official envelope. In fact the handwriting seems rather sloppy.

GABY—But who else would write me and for what reason?

DORILLA—Gabrielle, stop carrying on and open the damn letter. Oh, excuse my language.

GABY (Looks down at the letter and pushes it into her mother's hand.) I can't. You do it, Mama. Please.

DORILLA—Very well. But stop being so silly.

(Mrs. Richer tears open the letter and adjust her glasses. Slowly she begins to read it. At the same time light comes up over stage left to show George sleeping in his bunk, with a soldier, Ron Crandall, seated on a chair beside him. Crandall is writing.)

DORILLA—Dear Miss Richer, my name is Ron Crandall and I am...

CRANDALL—(picks up narrative from Dorilla)

...writing you this letter to tell you George is okay and getting better every day. I am one of his buddies on Battery B and he still is not in any shape to write. But he's been worried about your not hearing from him so he asked me to write this letter for him. I hope you can read it all right, as I am not very good at this writing stuff. George got malaria a couple of weeks ago and it hit him really fast. We had been getting pounded real hard night after night and none of us were getting any sleep. We were all walking around like zombies and sure enough, one night, George just folded up. We got him to the hospital tent real fast as he was burning up with fever. When the Doc saw him, he told us it was malaria and he had it bad.

For the next couple hours his fever just kept climbing and he was out of his head. So much so that we had to help the nurses hold him down. Miss Richer, he called out your name over and over again. Kept yelling he had to get back to you no matter what.

(Gaby starts to cry and Cecile hugs her for support.)

CECILE — It's okay, Gaby. George is okay. Go on, Mama, keep reading.

DORILLA—Right. Where was I? Oh, yes...here it is.

CRANDALL—Anyhow, his temperature got so high, things got real scary. They put him naked in a tub and filled it with ice. I ain't never seen nothing like it in my whole life. Poor old George started shaking and shivering so bad and his skin turned this weird gray color. But it worked, that ice bath. Along about sunrise his fever finally broke and the Doc announced he was past the critical stage. They got him back into a bunk and sure enough his breathing slowed down and he sort of went into a deep, peaceful sleep. When he came to, almost a day later, he was better but still weak as a baby. Which is how he has been these past weeks. The Doc says the only thing for him is lots of rest so that his body can get its natural strength back. I tell you, all us guys here in the battery were really praying for him to pull through.

DORILLA—(picking up letter from Crandall)Please do not stop writing as it is your letters every day that really pick him up. He reads them over and over again and they are the best medicine there is for him. Anyhow, he's wanted to write back but just couldn't get up his own stamina yet, so he got me to promise to write this letter. Which was my pleasure, as he is my best pal and there ain't nothing I wouldn't do for old George. So don't you go worrying no more. The malaria is all finished and he wants you to know he will write you as soon as he can. He also sends his love. Respectfully yours, Ronald W. Crandall, Private.

(Mrs. Richer folds up the letter and wipes a tear away from her own eyes. She gives the letter back to Gaby.)

DORILLA—There, now. You will remember to thank God when you go to bed tonight.

(Gaby takes the letter and hugs her mother.)

GABY—Oh, yes, Mama, I shall. I'll say the entire rosary. I'll say two of them.

CECILE—I will too, Mama.

DORILLA—That's good. Come along, now, both of you. It's almost dinner time and I need help in the kitchen. You know how Papa is when his dinner is not ready.

CECILE—Right. Even a dozen tubs of ice wouldn't put out that fire.

(They exit stage right.)

(George starts to wake up and Crandall puts down his writing pad.)

CRANDALL—Yo, sleeping beauty. How you doing?

GEORGE—Hi, Ron. Much better.

CRANDALL—You hungry?

GEORGE—Famished.

CRANDALL—I'll go find a nurse and rustle you up some chow. Oh, here. (He reaches down to pick up some letters on the floor by his chair.) Been holding all your mail while you were out of it.

GEORGE (Sitting up in bed.)—Thanks. Did you write Gaby, like I asked you?

CRANDALL—Sure did. Told her you'd been partying with those native girls and were on a two week drinking binge and that you'd write as soon as you sobered up.

GEORGE—Gee, thanks. You're a real pal.

CRANDALL—Shit, you'd only do the same for me.

(Another soldier enters stage right. He is carrying newspapers. It is Cpl.Armand Vachon from the USO scene.)

CPL VACHON—Hey, Fortier. How you doing?

GEORGE—Hi, Armand. I'm doing okay.

CRANDALL—Doc says he should be back with the outfit in another couple of days. Sooner if he leaves the nurses alone.

GEORGE—Ha, ha. Now about that chow.

CRANDALL—Oh, yeah. Be right back.

(Crandall exits stage left.)

CPL VACHON—I brought you some papers.

GEORGE—Thanks. How are things back at the base?

CPL VACHON—The usual. The Japs have been real quiet the past few weeks and not a single raid since the night after you got sick.

GEORGE—No shit. I wonder that means?

CPL VACHON (Taking the chair to sit down.) _

I know. Been lots of rumors floating around that the top brass is getting some new, super secret weapon ready to try out. Some kind of super bomb right out of Buck Rogers.

GEORGE—You think there is any truth to it?

CPL VACHON—Who the hell knows? But if there is, I sure hope they get off their butts and use it fast. At the rate this war is going now, we could be out here for the next ten years!

GEORGE—Don't even talk like that. Not even in joking. I just want to go home so bad I can taste it.

CPL VACHON—Amen to that, brother. Don't we all.

(Lights dim out over stage area and go up over Ron & Valerie.)

VALERIE—They were talking about the atomic bomb, weren't they?

RON—Right. Desperate to end the war, President Truman okayed its use and we dropped two of them. The first on Hiroshima, August sixth and a few days later another on Nagasaki. Both cities were leveled and the Japanese surrendered. World War Two was over. Mankind had survived the most brutal, inhuman conflict in its history.

VALERIE—And the boys came home.

RON—You bet. By the hundreds of thousands. My Dad returned sometime in mid September of 1945. It was quite the homecoming.

(Lights dim out over couple and go on over stage. John & Rose Fortier are at stage right, with Richard, in uniform, and Gaby and Cecile.)

Richard (Rushing to center stage and pointing to right.)—Look, here comes the bus! It's here!

ROSE—Oh, quiet down, Richard. We're not deaf. Oh, Papa. Do you see him?

JOHN—I think so. Yes! There he is..now. Oh, Mama, he looks so thin.

(George, carrying a duffle bag over his shoulder, enters stage right. Richard rushes to him and they shake hands happily as the rest of the family approaches.)

RICHARD—Hey, big brother!

GEORGE—Hey, little brother!

RICHARD—How you doing?

GEORGE—Right now, I'm doing great.

(Richard steps aside and George faces his parents. Rose rushes over and they hug, she kissing him all over his face.)

ROSE—Thank you, God. Thank you, God. My, baby. My sweet boy.

GEORGE—Mama. I missed you all so much.

(Rose finally lets him go and George and John face each other. John sniffles trying to hide his tears.)

GEORGE—Hello, Papa.

ROSE—For heaven's sake, will you two get on with it.

(John grabs George and they hug tightly.)

GEORGE—I love you, Papa.

JOHN—I know, boy. I'm..we're all so proud of you and your brothers. Welcome home.

(Rose taps John on the shoulder.)

ROSE—Leave some for Gabrielle.

JOHN—What? Oh, of course, Mama.

(John steps away from George. Gaby, with Cecile behind her, steps forward. She is nervous, not knowing how to act.)

GEORGE—Hello, beautiful.

(Gaby runs to his arms and they kiss.)

GABY—Oh, George.

(They break but still cling to each other. She is crying.)

GABY—You're here. You're really here!

GEORGE—I've dreamed of this moment for so long. I love you, Gaby Richer.

(They kiss again. A long kiss. Finally Rose coughs to get their attention.)

ROSE—Cough. Stop that now. There will be plenty of time for that and lots of other things. Now we have important things to do. A wedding needs planning.

GEORGE—OH. It does?

GABY—Yes. It does.

GEORGE—And do I have any say in the matter?

GABY—None whatsoever, sir. Except to say "I do" at the appropriate time. I let you go once, George Fortier. I promised God that if you came back to me, I'd never do that again.

(They kiss again.)

RICHARD—We could be here for a long time.

ROSE—All right, you two. Enough, is enough. A bus station is no place for sparking.

GEORGE (Finally releasing Gaby.)—I'm ready. I can't wait to see Somersworth and home again.

JOHN—It's pretty much the same way to you left it. Nothing much ever changes in Somersworth.

GEORGE—I know, Papa. Thank God for that.

(George spots Cecile and gives her a kiss on the cheek, causing her to blush.)

GEORGE—Hi, Cil. It's so good to see you again.

CECILE—Hey, you cut that out.

GABY—Right. Try to remember which Richer girl it is you're engaged to, lover boy.

(George offers his arm and she takes it.)

GEORGE—No chance of that, dear. Not ever.

(They all exit stage right. Lights fade out over stage and up over Ron and Valerie.)

VALERIE—How soon after were they married?

RON—A couple of months. December 1st to be exact.

VALERIE—Are we going to see it?

RON—Come on, now. Do you think I'd tell this whole story up to here and leave out the best part? (Ron sweeps his arm towards the stage.) We're going to a wedding.

(Lights go up over entire stage and the setting is St. Ignatius church again from Act I. It is much as we saw it previously with a few noticeable changes. Ray and his wife, Winnie, are there with three small children, the oldest being a girl about seven years old named Doris. The other two are boys. To the right of the stage, John Fortier is talking with George, Richard is behind them. Both George & Richard are in their army dress uniforms. Rose is talking with Dorilla and some of her children. Ron and Val walk into the scene—they are phantoms not visible to the other actors on the stage.)

VALERIE—Hmm. We've certainly been here before.

RON—Oh, yeah. Of course, quite a few things have changed since then.

WINNIE—Doris, will you sit still! I do not want you to get that new dress dirty.

DORIS—Yes, Mama. When is the wedding going to start?

WINNIE—Soon, dear. Just a few more minutes. Ray, keep those boys in their seats!

RAY—Yes, dear.

VALERIE—I see what you mean by changes.

RON—Doris was the oldest. The two boys are Ray Junior and Donald. They would later have two more, David and Nancy.

(Ron and Val walk towards John and George.)

RON—Of course the more things change, as the saying goes.

VALERIE—The more they stay the same.

JOHN—You know, George, this thing between a man and a woman...you know, the love thing.

GEORGE—I guess, Papa.

JOHN—Well, don't rush it, boy. You know, go easy and don't scare her. Gaby is a good girl, George. And she's going to be with you for the rest of your life.

GEORGE—I know, Papa. I know.

JOHN—Well, good. Because you don't have to do everything the first night.

GEORGE—Do what?

JOHN—You know. The sex thing.

GEORGE—Oh.

VALERIE—I don't believe this. Did that speech work any better this time around?

RON—Oh, God, yes. But not in the way my grandfather ever intended. You see, Dad was a virgin when he married Mom. All grandfather's speech did was scare the hell out of him. So much so that after they got settled into their hotel room that night, Mom says he locked himself in the bathroom and it took her nearly an hour to persuade him to come out.

VALERIE—You're making that up?

RON—Nope. It's the truth.

VALERIE—Your poor mother.

RON—To a degree, I suppose. But Mom always said, in love and sex, as well as everything else in their marriage, they learned from each other. That's something special.

(The wedding March begins to play and everyone goes to take their respective places. John and Rose sit down with Dorilla, while George and Richard stand by the raised dais where the priest has appeared from stage right. At stage left, a flower girl appears followed by Cecile and then Gaby and her father. They pause to wait while the others reach the altar.)

RON—My Dad was twenty-nine and my Mom had turned twenty-one the month before. There still eight years difference in their ages but it didn't matter anymore.

(Gaby turns and looks to pews at left back and a single light shines down on the area where we see her and Cecile -again as the two teen-age girls, excitedly whispering to each other as they did all those years ago- the light over them fades.)

MR.RICHER (Whispering to Gaby)—What's wrong, dear?

GABY—(Whispering back.) Nothing, Papa. I was just remembering the first time I ever saw George.

(They walk down the aisle and George steps forward. He and Mr. Richer shake hands and then Mr. Richer goes to sit with the others. Gaby and George turn; take a step up the dais and face the priest.)

PRIEST—Dearly beloved, we are gathered here in this holy place, to witness the union of this man and this woman.

(Priest continues but we do not hear him. Ron walks through the scene with Valerie.)

RON—So there you have it. How a thirteen year old girl spotted a twenty-one year old guy and fell in love.

VALERIE—What a great story. What happened to all of them?

RON—Uncle Richard met a girl from Massachusetts named Blanche, got married and had two boys, Richard Jr. and Roger. Aunt Cecile met a guy name Romeo Bennett, fell in love and started making babies like it was going out of style. By the time they were finished, they had eight. Seven girls and one boy.

VALERIE—Wow. That poor boy.

RON—Not really. Their house was filled with love. Shortly after the youngest was born, Uncle Romeo came down with cancer and died.

VALERIE—And Cecile had to bring up all those kids by herself?

RON—Yes. That she did a great job is evident by how close they still remain. Most of them are all married now and she has more grandkids than the population of some small towns.

(Ron and Val reach stage left and stop and look back at the altar where the priest is finishing the service.)

PRIEST—I now pronounce you man and wife. George, you may kiss your bride.

(George and Gaby kiss and then dash arm and arm down the aisle and exit stage left, followed by everyone else on stage. The lights fade out and Ron and Val walk to front center.)

RON—I was born nine months later. One of millions of post war babies throughout the world.

(As Ron speaks, the lights go on behind them—the church set having been removed to show an empty stage.)

RON — I was the oldest of four. We all grew up, married and had kids of our own. So George and Gaby had five grand children. They couldn't have been happier. Those kids grew up, married and produced another generation totaling seven beautiful boys and girls. Some of these are now already off to college and the family, like a mighty tree continues spread its roots throughout the world.

My mother and father had a very good life together. They continued to grow in their love for each other and that love sheltered all of us every single day of our lives. They had thirty years together. On Sept, 19, 1975, Dad became very sick and was rushed to the V.A. Hospital. Three days later, while in a coma, he died at the age of fifty-nine.

"I love you, Papa," was the last thing I said to him.

VALERIE - Tell them about the picture, Dear.

RON—Oh, right. A month before he died, Paul took a picture of Dad sitting in his favorite chair. When he had the photo developed, all of us were touched by how happy Dad looked. It seemed like he was completely content with himself. Valerie took the original and had copies made up and we gave one to each of my siblings.

Valerie put ours up on a wall in the den, then she surrounded it with dozens of pictures of our own kids, grand kids and friends. I love that wall.

One day, last year, while going past it, I stopped and looked at Dad's picture and all the others in orbit around it. I thought, isn't it amazing where love takes you?

I wrote this for my kids, who really didn't get to know the man all that much before he died. I wrote it for my family and to share it with all of you in the audience. I know it is not particularly unique or all that different from some of your own family stories. But here is the thing; you have to tell those stories. You have to tell them now, to your own children.

Because if you don't, you will rob them of their past and that would be a crime. Don't let that happen to you.

Now as for Mom, what about her, you ask? Well, at this writing, she is still going strong and I suspect just might outlive us all. After Dad passed away, she grieved for a long, long time. Finally she pulled herself out of her pain and got on with her life. How? Well, she started fulfilling her own dreams. She traveled to many exciting places from Africa to South America. She got involved with local politics and read the encyclopedia from cover to cover. Really, she did.

Then after a few years of this, friends got her to attend local singles dances where she met a nice guy named...

(Valerie touches Ron's arm.)

VALERIE—Ahem. Dear?

RON—Yes? What?

VALERIE—That's another story. Isn't this one finished?

RON—You're right. (To the audience again) Excuse me. Thank you for coming. I hope you liked our play and will tell your friends about it. Take care and God bless each and every one of you. Good-bye.

VALERIE—Nicely done, my love.

(She and Ron kiss and then begin walking off stage as the lights start to fade behind them.)

VALERIE—You know, you're just like your father.

RON—Really? How so?

VALERIE—You're such a lousy dancer.

CURTAIN FALLS

HISTORY & RIGHTS

WHERE LOVE TAKES YOU
By Ron Fortier

Was first performed in Springvale, Maine by the Sanford Stage Company on 10th Aug, 2001 and was directed by Mary Stair and David Goodwin.

ORIGINAL CAST

Companies or schools wishing to produce the play should contact the author directly.

Ron Fortier
2519 S. Shields #104
Fort Collins, CO 805260-1855

www.ingramcontent.com/pod-product-compliance
Lightning Source LLC
Chambersburg PA
CBHW071455070426
42452CB00039B/1361